# What Black Delirious Daylight Sets you Forward in the Boat

ROBIN WYATT DUNN

JOHN OTT

2017

San Diego, California

Cover art by Jael Harrington

ISBN - 978-1-940830-20-9

LOC - 2017XXXXXX

By Robin Wyatt Dunn

POETRY
*Poems from the War*
*Science Fiction: a poem!*
*Remarriages*
*Sunsborne*
*Wine Country*
*Debudaderrah*


FICTION
*Los Angeles, or American Pharaohs*
*My Name is Dee*
*Fighting Down into the Kingdom of Dreams*
*Line to Night Island*
*A Map of Kex's Face*
*Julia, Skydaughter*
*Conquistador of the Night Lands*
*White Man Book*
*Colonel Stierlitz*
*Black Dove*
*City, Psychonaut*
*2DEE*


PLAYS
*Last Freedom*


FILMS
*A Wilderness in Your Heart*
*Party Games*
*American Messenger*

*for Steve*

I love you
like the drifts of wood
earning their ordure in the black sea.

imbue me
I am here
weathered in your lee

to hear your voice

now we are beginning

I have called you;
to learn the ages of your eyes
they are many;
too many for me;
how can anyone live with so many ages?

Like the wood would stop growing
to fold itself under the ground.

where are the pages of your step?
I've not seen them.
Infinite, but where is even one?

I could have moved it, maybe
when I was drunk
and the wind was in my eyes

magnet for my arm to your ankle

I love you for coarse
the embodiment of dumb
it's dumb, the earth
dumb, the poem
it will never speak
it has no light
nor any thought of any
it shudders in the thunder of the bomb

I bomb you
with love

from the sky
I rain bombs of love


great and terrible love
shining bombs
holy love
igniting your house
and your eyes

I am god, at least in this moment,
sent to terrify your city
with all of our love
white hot and shaking the ground
unbelievable and eternal love
shall root thee to your spot

so to mark your face with the wisdom of it

no one shall burn like me
I am only the poet

Strap me in
for twenty hours
the vibrating engines will numb me to sleep.

drifting east
to the renewal of our guns
undulous, napping

I turn away for the mirror of my dream
(somewhere in a dark apartment with a murderous man)

Civilian he no know the city
Civilian he no know the right
I got two cents and a shark says I'm the mark for the hour

Gut me with your guts
And strew me around the place
I'm a poet, I can take it
I stick readily to walls and bar stools
I am residue
I am a glommer
And I can reglom too;
When you're done;
and all thought of running is fled
I shall surround you with my lines

Don't fence me in;
I'll fence you in
for every fence knows how much he can get
for every sharpened word

Burn me when it's close to dark
and the spark of the arc of the day brims over
and sucks you up inside

I'm one inside the dark

I'm the cummerbund of love
Ridiculous,
Iniquitous,
Flat and caped and silk,
A rape of love,
A band of love,
A shield:
A sword:

a wedding without fame
or name
or place
or memory

wedding the flashing sight of forty-five
with the years of plenty in the dust

To you anonymous lover
Unknown lover
Drunken lover
Bearded lover
Holy lover
Dimpled lover
Young lover
Aging lover
Tired lover
Black lover

All the sea
is meant for thee
after I am gone

But the sea isn't enough
I'm still here;
Trying to remember your number

My father is a rock man
Like a small mountain
Curved and black.

he will tell you everything you want to know about rocks.
How they got there,
and where they are going.

He doesn't know where he is going,
But he knows where the rocks are.

he is standing forty feet from the reddish outcrop
        in Los Angeles county
where we were born
where my grandfather fled to from Brooklyn
where all the lies can run over you like water
a strange and polluted water
but holy—
a medicine.

we are gnomon to American sundial
unmoving
marking the angle to stars
and insisting:

now is the time

My father is a rock man
and his love is like a rock:
tall, and brittle.
Reddish.
It smells like dust, and loam.

I am leaving Los Angeles.
The only city I've ever loved.

Over the estuary of the night,
Traffic is shrieking at me
In its holy voice.

The gods of Hollywood are chanting
in heavily accented English
all the titles I never earned

Begin to love with me
and you'll see quickly what we must leave out
any of the reasons, the whys
any of the locations, or the directions
any of the words
words are loveless and love is wordless and my advice
is to stay rooted to your spot
and let the moon move over you,
since the moon is meant for lovers,
and since its agony describes a music few can hear,
actuarial to the heart
horrible divine sent to usher you into the play:

curtains up
lights on
cue the music

sing, motherfucker
with my knife to your back

with my knife to your back,
I am your love

sent to this poem with your name
Leaven me
to coast round the night

over the stars
and the windows of the city

tell me the hour
and the minute

and I'll give you hell

flash it right on the page
a finely machined rage
with the sanction of the state,
a face to terrify the skin of the earth.

I man the minute with my muse
a hearse a ruse a stinking dream
a god or godlet
a man or woman
a rock or a poem

a song

you

bilious and alive
burgeoning, and magical
a worldly demon for me to worship
with my eyes and hands

the muse is a wreck
a stinking wreck
irresistible

someone else's dream
carefully constructed
inside the lab
mercury and nembutal
luxury and ruth

the truth skids under the door
sweating and bleeding
looking around for the principal

it's broken
& in love
it's truthful
(a poem)

it's me
or like me
me when I'm me not me
this me
that me
some me
most of me
a little of me

not like Walt Whitman,
simply because he lived in 1855—

trembling arms
numb legs
a brain on fire
leaded eyes
chapped lips
a cold penis
an ant moving slow over my left foot

blacken me and burn
the root and the route to earth

the decision to love
like an old whisker
a shabby contract
a trembling majesty
a dead queen in a beautiful temple
the run of the muck of the steed of your youth
still improbably delicious
wracked runt and wired to the max
for the chance at the truth

or this part of it we set aside,
a broken budda with his ash tray
and his gleamy smile

golden trauma

love me
like an axe
trembling viking axe

no storm shall know my name
even you will have forgotten it
in our dreams

love me
though I am easy to please
love me
though I am ornery
love me
though I might kill you
love me
though it is dangerous
love me
through the spite of it all
through the galactic charter session
with nerds from all corners of the earth
eagerly setting up their dungeon and dragons sessions
love me
after the earth has moved away
from out and beneath our feet

love me now

a command
like so many men-drinks,
is delicious and nutritious and so much fun,
which is to say,
a hell of a lot of work,
and a big spell to sell,
Merlin on crack cocaine,
Mordred on ketamine.

a command lays the path
for the weight of the act
troopers set their studs to the mark
raise the eaves of the church
hang the trowels over your porch
Shakespeare arrives for his dream
little bells dangling from his robe

love me for dreams
and for the spastic quality of my awareness
and for the umbilicus I still grasp
inside galactic center.

love me for cheap
after the movie theater's shut
after the town's shut down
after the king is asleep
and the queen's at war
love me over the park
in a cheap bench
stuck in a tree
a squirrel house
not totally shielded from the rain

Give it a figure like a man
black as the rain
over the blankets

give it a figure like a woman
black as night
quiet like night
deadly

give it a lingering regard
a few details

then forget all of them
decide to love anyway

the figure of you

I'll give you a hat
and a ruse
I'll give you shoes
bat and boots
cat and hooves
night

and night

all the nightmares come out to play
with their many arms and voices
like lingering cyclopses thrumming in the dark
over the sky
the universe

I'll give you a poem
and send it to you

write the day
and the broken earth
write the mast
and the shaken verse of the sky over your face

tell me it was worth it
was it worth it, all those years,
when you spoke my name?

I'm still here

I love you you've forgotten
and I love the you I've forgotten
and you forgot to love
inside your golden orange
and your radiant despair

I'm there too,
holding the corners of your curtains
looking for a way to dislodge you from the
couch

each dance you do
a flat rat
in a lonely maze
made by a delirious architect in a far off city

my remote control is not working

I love you, a broadcast frequency
a channel
cut earth for pharaoh, moving into the reeds

inundate my roots

black night and baleful visage
modern equipment for a grim-frocked marriage
pageant to the moon

dance with my body

I've been practicing Michael Jackson's thriller move
with my arm
making it a robot limb
repeatedly agitating the air over your head

my desire, as embodied in the robot limb of my arm,
floods with fluid.
works the music.
jacks the sound and through it,
in the interim twilight
my voice is a caul over the sky
the room

the pool of the city

cut me and shimmer sad to the member maddened sound of
        druid bones and cut stones
magic hours and milled music
mud music
married to music
brunt boned harmonies and pageants chaos-curled to know the
        moment to note
the step
the arc
the weight and the bow to the bruise of love
the howl of the earth and the map of your face

move through to love
to chart its earth
the burnt crust of the scone
in your abandoned oven

move through to love
to batten down its hatch
and ship it to australia
where the aborigines have been practicing their necromancy

when I arrive
unwrap me
a zombie,
a seed,
lurking under the note of the dove

(coo coo)

young people are so interesting
each of them a movie star
in a low budget film
with minimal makeup
and a james dean john steinbeck horizon
broken automobile
and narrow eyes

cutting a notch into the mountain

young people parturate the bliss
of the move of the stones of the body
barking the mad orders of a clock residing under our roads

young people barter the husk of the owned
for the fleur and flyers round your head

burning galactic memories in your flesh

I am alone
like a poem is alone
pissing and moaning in a precise decanter
an encampment
in a lonely valley
beset with snow, and wind, and a whole lot of sky

I am alone
like the earth is alone
watching the sun
for the reasons
and the end of the lure:
the hook

hook me down
to the darkened down
of your arm

dove me lurking well under your ash sky
for the mountains and ranges of your muse
sent to praise my poem
from your harrowing sky

I like it
when the dag dangles dandies on the freeway
and when the buses move bodies like stones
bumbling alone
knocking about in a park
numbing the regard of the blank street
to the shining sky

I like it
when the black sunday
cuts to the red monday
and the gallow stalk of the hour
hums like a loveable killer
walking through woods

I like it
when the barter stock brays at my hand
and the bleak festering wound of the city
            teaches me knowledge I need.


I like it
when we roll through the park without music
but hear music inside

a yellow river Danube
conducting Marco Polo to China

It's black and blue
my you
thundering love
it's wracked and used, my love
my you

when the mark stops
and the bad omen hums
and the breed makes his mark
on my thumb
on my hand
on my forehead
on my love

bury me under the bones of the hearth
of your hands

and fling me into the dark
to be stars

it's round and fragrant
a fruit
it's long and armed
mendicant
luring the truth to its tongue
with the moment

break free
and fast
cut the line and push off:
this Mississippi pulses with the bard of your ale
singing the system still to be
still to be mine

sing me the system of your park
your dark divines
your milky substance striated and filtered
harbored wet crumby and luminescent
a starry ark, bulbous jellyfish
under the surface of the river

sing me the reasons for your lark
over the tree tops
when I saw your face smile
some woman I have never seen
building the reasons for poems
and the shape of the freeway

the scent of the freeway too:
black cadences
locusts of dark avenues
and the shape of the infinite California dark

Sing me the reasons
though there are none
any more than colors are reasons
shot through the dark

red and mercury and ochre
the cambodian yellow
the piston of the drift of your eye

shift my body over the scent of your clementine
scrape the knees of my festering wound
shape the augury of my bones

I augur well

I am auguring your sky

I augur the branch of your sea

and the melancholy deep of your arm

your wintery arm

I augur well
the mandate of your year
it is enlightened
it is embossed
with the cut of the pull of your gravity.

I augur well
the wrap of the deep
under your well
I have seen it pulling you over the tiger forest
and into the black eye of the future

I have seen it deliver you to a city I've never seen
Neon and ash
winter colors and catholic curves

sing me the rapture of your eaves
under your hair

Blacken me to use
under your door
freshen me to bruise
the lock of your door

usher me to cull
the mark of your divorce

deck me the harm of your regret
over your table
deal me out

deal me out for your reward
I am coming

deal me out for your enlarged reward
a million ears
for a million arms
not in a million years will the shattering light startle me again
you shatter it
over your head

deal me out for your enlarged reward
it is coming in grass
in leaves
in orders from the mountains of trees
ringing about you

here in Hollywood we have set bars
for our Jewish prison
made of wood
made for burning.

there is nothing more beautiful than a Jewish prison
made of wood
arranged with furniture and gourds.

let me see your breasts
for our final rapture
in a yellow cafe.

I have flown over the city,
looking for your name,
because of your breasts.

in our Jewish prison,
we can see stars between the columns of briars
and drink wine to celebrate the silence of the earth.

I have seen you looking at the art on the walls,
wondering when it will be me.

I love you shaking the earth in the city
sharpening your coil in the cafe in the city
under blue mosaics
next to spinning dreamcatchers
while the skinny waiters look on in fear
while the gay diners open their mouths
and the sky falls silent
for the murders of the earth

I have seen you burn the earth
with your eyes
young and unrepentant
greedy for the color of sin
over your forehead.

I love you setting the cafe to wait
for everything to move

I loved you when I slept above the lake (now drained)
and when the neighbor man shouted his strange dreams into our houses.
you were a cavernous butterfly
all colors
fluttering in the dark

strange butterfly,
redeem me,
for it is the city that made me break so many promises.
I didn't know there were so many promises to break.

I didn't know that I could see them break
one after the other
like a civil demonstration, of a new weapon.

I know what we made.
even though it doesn't have a name,
it has a color.
sort of an insect color; shiny.

I should make it into a cape,
And wear it around the city.

Well, we're always losing.
I wrote a poem titled "life is losing."
And what I meant by that poem was:
life is this beautiful process of losing everything
and everything you lose will make you even more beautiful.
But no one seemed to understand that about the poem.
Perhaps it was very badly written.

I am losing you,
in order to be free.
Even though freedom is something that can only exist with others.
Solitude is, logically, the ultimate prison.

I am losing you,
to right the hang of the door of the mountain
for when the pied piper wants to go into it,
he will need a good door,
and so will you,
when you want to go into the mountain dark,
to recite poems.

I'll ramp up
the evening and the sky
I'll ramp up
the damp goodnight
I'll ramp up
the luminous dark
to drink you in.

I'll ramp up
the arduous crush of the days
and the weight of the sky over the water
to see you better.

I'll ramp up the water and the bays
and the clouds over the water
the storms over your eyes
I'll ramp up
the power and regret
of the shift beneath your weight
and the band underneath your hat
which had been fraying when you bought it

I'll ramp up the light and fix
of the styx of earth you're drifting in
till midnight catches us
and turns us into splashes of green

I'll ramp up, for you,
The battle cry of the city.

Who has heard the battle cry of a city?
When was the last time we heard it?
It must be so beautiful.

I'll ramp up, for you,
The powerful grace of the army of poets
swarming about us
insisting and resisting the turns of their fate
lovers in washrooms
ashes in space

I'll ramp up, for you
The moon of my regard
and the space of your sound
your sounding night
lulling the trout to sleep

Break the knot of love
into two
and from that little Gordian treasure,
make the ocean move,
to fill the earth between you,
A godawful disaster,
rich with meaning and reward.

fill up with two
the harbor of your thoughts
with three
with four

the undine wreckage of your bodies
spinning into the dark

spin me in darkness
where I cannot find you
except by your eyes

love's easy, of course,
like getting drunk and forgetting to pay the bill.
we keep track of it like your feet keep track of your weeks,
waiting for the right moment to hurt.

if we can regard love as a kind of stunt device,
the machina in deus ex machina,
it's fair to say mine lights up at the appropriate time
in the appropriate seat
with a dim blue light
after the sake is poured
and the conversation is too loud
and I have bored you completely.

I unfold for you
Like a cheap brochure
In a tired tourist shop
Blasted by Mediterranean light.

Inside the faded pictures,
I am waving,
Dignified,
In a ridiculous costume,
And demonstrating one of my distinct cultural dances.

I unfold for you
Like a poem
A weaponized simulation of reality
Set to stir your feet.

Inside the simulation,
I am breaking windows, carefully,
With a hammer.

I like *langsam* better than longing,
Because it's German,
And because it has an 's' in it.
*Langsam* is stickier than longing,
It sounds like what it is:
A wet butt.

I am rowing
With you behind me.

Russia is named for 'row':
That's what 'Rus' means.

The stars too are seas.
Turning over us in waves.

Heed me, to the north star,
And bend east,
Into the river,
Into the marsh and the reeds and the ducks and the cities fantastical,
Underneath our oars.

I am rowing
Inside the imagination.
These waters are not infinite,
But they are very large.

Is the imagination smaller than the universe, or greater?
Is it dangerous to measure?

Our scabbards and sextants know our purposes are small but noble
They cleave to our hands
Like children.

Wave with me,
At the passing light,
For I have seen you there too,
Somewhere in the death I have been.

I am a writer
But you write me

## ABOUT THE POET

Robin Wyatt Dunn lives in a state of desperation
engineered by late capitalism, within which his
mind is a mere subset of a much larger hallucina-
tion wherein men are machines, machines are men,
and the world and everything in it are mere dreams
whose eddies and currents poets can channel briefly
but cannot control. Perhaps it goes without saying
that he lives in Los Angeles.